Celebrations
HARVEST

Hilary Lee-Corbin

Wayland

Celebrations

Christmas   New Year
Easter   Hindu Festivals
Hallowe'en   Jewish Festivals
Harvest   Muslim Festivals

All words that appear in **bold** are
explained in the glossary on page 46

First published in 1989 by
Wayland (Publishers) Limited
61 Western Road, Hove
East Sussex BN3 1JD, England

British Library Cataloguing in Publication Data
Lee-Corbin, Hilary
  Harvest and Thanksgiving – (Celebrations)
  1. Harvest festivals, – For children
  I. Title   II. Series
  394.2'683

ISBN 1 85210 741 3

Phototypeset by Kalligraphics Ltd, Horley, Surrey

Printed and bound in Italy by G. Canale & C.S.p.A., Turin

Contents

Why have a harvest festival?

In the past, most people lived in villages and worked on farms. They grew crops and kept animals. Cows gave people milk and meat. Sheep gave them wool as well as meat. Pigs and chickens were kept to provide people with food, too.

4

This farmer and his family grow their own food, but most people today buy their food from shops.

Years ago, farmers did not know about feeding the soil to get a good harvest. If too little rain fell, the crops died. Too much rain could spoil a harvest. Sometimes animals died from diseases.

In those days, there were no shops to go to. If the harvest was bad, people had no food to eat. They sometimes starved.

So, when the harvest was good, people were happy. When all the crops had been harvested, everyone had a party. This was called a harvest festival.

Harvests around the world

Every day of the year, a harvest is being gathered somewhere in the world. This is a wheat harvest in the USA.

In northern lands, like Britain and North America, harvests ripen in summer. This is from June to September.

The grape harvest in Greece is in November.

In southern lands, like New Zealand and Australia, summer comes between December and March. That is the time when they have their harvest.

Some parts of the world just have wet seasons and dry seasons. Seeds are sown in the wet season and harvested in the dry season.

In other places, where there is no long dry season, crops are grown and harvested all year round.

In Britain, one of the first harvests is the strawberry harvest. It starts in June. One of the last crops to be harvested is the potato crop, in November.

Some crops can be harvested very quickly. If you sow mustard and cress seed in a saucer, you can have your own harvest in three weeks.

Crops like maize can be grown and harvested quickly. Maize is used to feed farm animals. These Spanish farmers are collecting maize.

When there is a good harvest, the shops have plenty of food to sell.

Some crops are harder to grow than others. People are very happy when all their crops grow well.

But even easy crops can have bad years. The weather may be wrong, or insects may attack the plants. So farmers are always pleased when their crops are successful. That's why, in countries all over the world, they like to have a harvest festival after a year of hard work.

Harvests in other times and places

Long ago, farmers must have wondered about the life in the seed they sowed. How did it get there and what made it grow?

In those days, people believed in many gods and goddesses. They decided that it was the gods who helped the seeds to grow into plants. So, when they held their harvest festival, farmers thanked the gods for their help.

This is Ceres, the Roman goddess of farming. Her name gives us the word 'cereal'.

10

Farmers also had to make sure their gods would help them again in the coming year. So they made up songs and prayers to keep their harvest gods happy.

This picture shows farm workers in Egypt gathering in **corn** long ago.

In South America, the **Incas** had a harvest festival at the time of the maize harvest. They ▶ had feasts to thank the sun god for their harvest.

People made up stories about the harvest gods. The Romans made up stories about Ceres, their corn goddess.

One story says that Ceres' daughter, Proserpine, was carried off to be the Queen of the Underworld. After a lot of trouble she was allowed to spend six months of the year on Earth with her mother and six months as a prisoner in the Underworld. Her six months in the Underworld were winter, and her six months on Earth were summer.

North American Indians believed the rain god
brought water for the crops and the sun god gave
warmth and light.

In Egypt, when the flood season came, people
thought their god Osiris had come back to them.

13

Celebrating the harvest

Let's have a harvest festival

Brightly coloured clothes are worn by people at harvest fairs in the USSR. In many countries, churches are filled with flowers, fruit and vegetables.

14

People bring gifts to church for the harvest festival. They may bring flowers, fruit or vegetables from their gardens. ▶ Not many people grow their own food, so in cities most of the gifts come from shops.

People also bring eggs, jam and tins of food. In many churches a lump of coal and a glass of water are put with the gifts. This is to show that these are also gifts from God. There is often a big loaf in the shape of a wheat sheaf, too.

When everybody helped with the harvest

In Britain and many parts of North America the corn harvest comes at the end of July. Long ago, men cut the wheat by hand. Women gathered up the stalks and tied them into **sheaves**.

The sheaves were stored in tent-shaped clumps called **stooks** to dry. After about two weeks, the stooks were built into haystacks. Later on, in winter, they were **threshed**. This means taking the **grain** away from the straw. The grain was then ground into flour to make bread.

The harvest was finished when all the haystacks
had been built.

Harvest was a very busy time. Everyone who lived
nearby helped. Even children were kept busy. Some
led the horses which pulled the wagons. Some
helped to stand the sheaves into stooks. Everyone
worked all day long. The harvest might take six
weeks to gather. If it rained, it took longer.

Before we had machines, the corn was cut by hand
using sharp **scythes** or **sickles**.

17

The end of harvest

Each farm in a village tried hard to be the first to finish its harvest. The farmers wanted all the haystacks to be built before it rained.

When the last sheaf was picked up, all the men would join a special 'harvest shout', ending with 'Hip, hip, hooray!'

The shout told the workers on other farms that this farm had finished its harvest. Everyone would be very happy that their hard work was over for another year.

The next day there would be a big party called a Harvest Home feast. It was often held in a barn. Lots of food would be eaten and there would be beer and cider to drink. Then the harvesters would dance and sing. ➡

The Lord of the Harvest was the man who told each worker what to do. He drove the last wagon home, and sat next to the farmer at the Harvest Home feast.

The gleaners

Harvest Home feasts sometimes had a Harvest Queen. Usually she was the wife or the girlfriend of the Lord of the Harvest. She tied the sheaves of corn for him.

This **gleaner** has a sheaf of corn in one hand and a sickle in the other.

As soon as a field was cleared of sheaves, the women and children used to begin **gleaning**. Gleaning means picking up the stray ears of corn that are left in the field after the sheaves are gathered. The ears are the part of the plant that contains the seeds.

A poor woman could sometimes glean enough corn for her family to last the winter. After the harvest, she rubbed the grain out of the corn, and took it to the miller who ground it into flour. At home she would make bread and bake it in her oven.

Corn dollies

Corn dollies were an important part of the harvest. They were made out of straw.

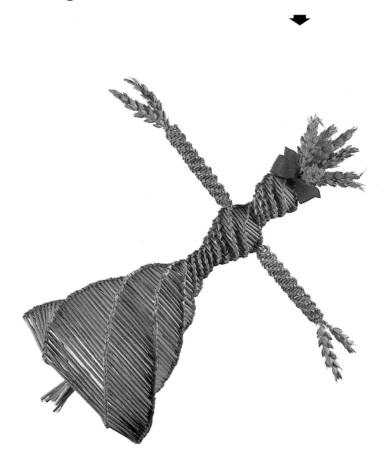

Corn dollies had to be made out of the last straw to be cut. This is because people believed the 'corn goddess' lived in it.

22

When the harvesters started to cut the corn, they
thought they were robbing the corn goddess of her
home. So, when they came to the end of the harvest,
they thought she was hiding in the few stalks that
were left. They carefully cut these stalks, hiding
their faces so that the goddess could not see them.
This man is holding up the last corn of the harvest.

Corn dollies were made from these stalks. They
were put on the table at the Harvest Home feast.
When the fields were ploughed in January, the corn
dollies were put back into the soil. Farmers believed
this would help to make the next harvest a good one.

Thanksgiving in North America

The first Thanksgiving

Many years ago, some people called the Pilgrim Fathers sailed from England to North America. Here you can see a picture of them on their ship, the *Mayflower*. When they got to America it was too late to plant any seeds, so that winter they had very little to eat. The Native American Indians were friendly, though, and brought them food.

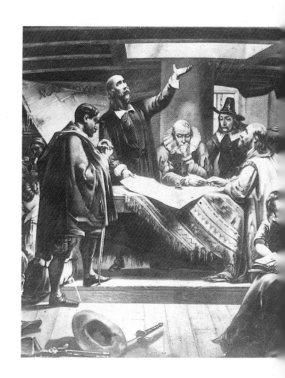

In the spring they planted seeds and at the end of the summer there was a good harvest. So they thought they would have a festival of Thanksgiving.

They had a feast with fish, geese, ducks, turkey and lots of fruit. The Native Americans also joined in.

Later, when other people arrived in that part of America, they thought a festival was a good idea. So Thanksgiving was held every year.

Thanksgiving Day

Over the years, all Americans began to celebrate
Thanksgiving Day. When the Americans wanted to
give thanks to God for winning their wars, they did
it on Thanksgiving Day. This is now held on the
fourth Thursday in November. Canada also has a
Thanksgiving Day, which is held in October.

Many people watch sports on Thanksgiving Day.
They enjoy having a day's holiday from work.

Thanksgiving Day is a happy time when American
families share a big meal. Most people have turkey
and lots of other good things to eat. Some go to
church and thank God for the happiness of family
life over the past year.

27

Harvest festivals around the world

Australia, Fiji and the Far East

Many years ago, people sailed from Britain and went to live in Australia and New Zealand. There people have harvest festivals which are like those in Britain. They have their festivals in church and people bring gifts of flowers, fruit and vegetables. But their harvest is in February or March, not August or September.

On the island of **Fiji**, coconuts, rice, **yams**, bananas and sugar cane are grown. The islanders ▶ have a harvest festival like those in Britain.

Australian farmers keep many sheep. At sheep
shearing time they have a festival. Shearing means
cutting the wool from the sheep.

These dancers are at a Japanese harvest festival
called the New Taste Festival. It is held on
23 November. At midnight the Emperor of Japan
gives thanks for the first fruit of the harvest.

Japan's harvest is at about the same time as harvest in Britain. They grow some of the same crops as British farmers, but they also grow rice.

The Japanese pray to a rice god at their festival. On the festival day everyone sits down to a feast with lots of wine made from rice.

In countries where **Buddhism** is the religion, a great festival is held at the first full moon after the rainy season. These girls live on the island of Bali in ▶ the Indian Ocean. They are taking harvest gifts to the temple. The gifts will be given to the poor.

India, Africa and the Middle East

There are many farmers in India and Africa who grow all their own food. When they have a good harvest they give thanks to their gods.

In India, evil spirits are driven away at harvest time. A little corn is taken from each house. Then young men beat the seed and hope to chase the evil spirits away. This is an Indian thanksgiving festival. ➡

Some people in Africa give the first vegetables and fruit of each harvest to the gods. Then they eat any food left over from last year's harvest. Only then are they allowed to taste the first of the new harvest.

In some Arab lands they put the last handful of wheat into the grave of someone who has died. Then they say 'May God give us back the wheat from the dead.' This is very like what people in Europe used to do with corn dollies.

33

The Festival of
First Fruits

Sometimes festivals are held at the beginning of the harvest. In some Christian lands a Festival of the First Fruits was held. This was to thank God for the ripe harvest, before it was gathered in.

In the Bible, farmers are told to put their first fruits in a basket and present them to a priest. In England long ago, people took the first ears of wheat and ground them into flour. With the flour they made little round loaves and took them to church to be blessed.

This festival became known as 'Loaf mass'. 'Mass' means festival. As the years went by it came to be known as **Lammas**. Lammas was on 1 August.

Jewish harvest festivals

Jews have two harvest festivals, one for the wheat harvest and the other for fruit. The first is called the feast of Pentecost.

Jewish churches, called synagogues, are decorated with plants and flowers for Pentecost. Jewish families have a feast on that day. This synagogue window shows harvest fruit and vegetables.

The fruit harvest festival is called Succoth. It lasts a week. Synagogues are decorated with plants and flowers. The people go there to thank God for the harvest.

36

During Succoth, families eat in a *sukkah,* a special kind of tent. Years ago, Jewish people used to live in tents like those when they went away from home to pick fruit.

Other harvests

Forest harvests

Long ago, whole families went to gather the forest's harvest. Nuts, acorns, berries and mushrooms were all collected. Nuts and acorns were mixed with flour to make bread. Berries were made into jam. Sometimes roots were dug up which could be made into medicine.

Today we do not collect acorns or roots but we still pick nuts and berries.

People often had a feast when the forest harvest was gathered. Because the harvests were gathered in autumn, the feasts became mixed up with the saints' days that came at that time of year. The saint that people remembered most in autumn was Saint Michael. His special day is on 29 September.

The harvest of animals

Every year the fields had a crop of grain and the fruit trees had a crop of fruit. Every year, also, the farm animals had a crop of young ones. Cows, sheep, pigs and chickens all had babies.

40

In the autumn, farmers looked at their animal harvest. They had to keep enough animals to give another crop of young ones next year. The rest were sold at special fairs. One of the biggest animal fairs in England was at Winchester. It was called Saint Giles' Fair.

All the animals that were to be eaten in the winter were killed on the same day, Saint Martin's Day, 11 November. Big fires were lit and everyone feasted on fresh meat.

Today, most farmers sell their animals at markets. This prize bull is being shown at a show in New Zealand.

The harvest of the sea

For people who lived by the sea there was another harvest. Their harvest was fish. Around Britain the main time for fishing was between May and October. While the men were out fishing, the women had to harvest the corn. When the fish were brought home they had to be salted so that they would last through the winter. While all this was going on, there was no time for festivals.

In many lands, fishing boats are blessed before going out to sea. Fishing can be dangerous if the weather is stormy. When the harvest of the sea is good, the fishermen and their families live well.

In some parts of Britain, fishing festivals used to be held. In the Shetland Isles, to the north of Scotland, deep-sea fishing ended at Lammas, on 1 August. When all the boats were safely home, a harvest feast was held.

On the Isle of Man, herring fishing finished much later. The fishermen's harvest festival (called a boat supper) was held on 20 December.

Tomorrow's harvest festival

Today, if we visit a wheat field at harvest time, we shall not find lots of people in it, as there used to be. There will be just one man on a **combine harvester** and one man with a tractor and trailer, taking the grain back to the barn. That will be all. Only a very few people now earn their living from farming. Machines do most of the work.

Most of us do not have to grow our own food or look after farm animals. We buy what we need from a shop or supermarket. Tea comes from India or Sri Lanka, sugar from Jamaica. Milk and butter come from cows that may be living in Ireland, Denmark or France. The wheat in our bread may have come from the USA or Canada.

44

In the past, people held thanksgiving festivals for the harvests of their own fields. Today we celebrate the harvests of the whole world. We must thank not only the people who grow the food, but also those who bring it to us by land, sea and air.

Glossary

Buddhism An eastern religion founded by a man called the Buddha.

Combine harvester A machine for cutting and threshing grain.

Corn Cereal plants, such as wheat, oats, barley and maize.

Corn dollies Little figures made out of the last wheat to be cut at harvest time.

Fiji An island in the Pacific Ocean.

Gleaners People who gathered the stray pieces of wheat left behind by the harvesters.

Grain The seed of a plant such as wheat or barley.

Incas South American Indians.

Lammas Loaf Mass, a festival held on 1 August.

Scythe A large curved blade on a long handle, used to cut crops in the fields.

Sheaves Bundles of corn tied together.

Sickle A tool with a curved blade and short handle. It was used to cut crops or grass.

Stook Group of sheaves stacked together in the field.

Threshing Beating corn, by hand or machine, to take the grain away from the rest of the plant.

Yams Large vegetables rather like potatoes.

Books to read

Festivals by B. Birch (Macdonald, 1984)

Festivals by Jeanne McFarland (Macdonald Educational, 1981)

Festivals and Celebrations by Rowland Purton (Basil Blackwell, 1983)

Festivals and Celebrations by Kathleen Elliott (Young Library, 1984)

Index

Acknowledgements

The publisher would like to thank all those who provided pictures on the following pages: ET Archive Ltd. 13, 40; BBC Hulton Picture Library 23; R. Burton/Bruce Coleman Limited 44; Mary Evans Picture Library 18, 20, 22, 35; Sally & Richard Greenhill 15; Sonia Halliday Photographs 36; The Mansell Collection 19, 21; Peter Newark's Western Americana 25; Ann & Bury Peerles 32; PHOTRI 6, 24, 26 photographer B. Kulic, 28, 41; Picturepoint Ltd. 30, 43; Ronald Sheridan's Photo-Library 10, 11, 12; TASS 14, 45; TOPHAM 31 photographer C. Osbourne; Malcolm S. Walker 34, 37; ZEFA 27 photographer A. Hubrich, 39 photographer W. Lummer.